SPIRIT OF THE MAYA

• GUY GARCIA •

SPIRIT OF THE MAYA

A BOY EXPLORES HIS PEOPLE'S MYSTERIOUS PAST

PHOTOGRAPHS BY **TED WOOD**

WALKER AND COMPANY **NEW YORK**

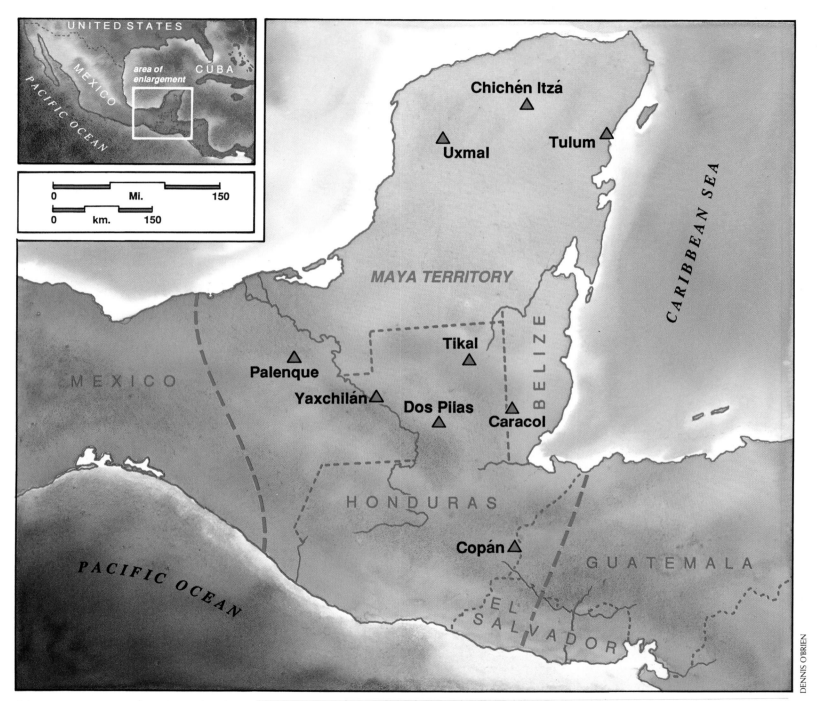

Maya territory and major ruin sites.

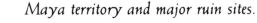

INTRODUCTION

Their universe was protected by giant spirits, called *bacabs* (bah CAHBs), who held up the four corners of the sky. Other gods ruled the rain, the seasons, and the corn. There were gods of the day and of the night. The gods could be kind or cruel; they could give life or take it away. To keep the gods happy, the Maya offered them prayers and held great ceremonies led by priests who wore masks and feathers, danced, and played sacred music.

At the height of their civilization the Maya ruled a vast empire that covered much of what is now southern Mexico, Guatemala, Honduras, and Belize. They lived in bustling cities and built towering stone pyramids to honor the gods and their dead ancestors. They believed that time progressed in twenty-year cycles and that one day the world as they knew it would come to an end.

Then, around 900 A.D., the Maya kings vanished and their cities were abandoned. Today, more than a thousand years later, millions of Maya remain in the lands of their ancestors. Most of them live in modern cities and speak Spanish like everyone else. But not all have forgotten their past. The Lacando'n (Lah kahn DOHN) Indians and a few other Maya peoples have kept their heritage alive. They still speak their native language and honor the lords who built the great pyramids. The old ways live on in their hearts, and the gods dwell in the realm of their dreams.

When the sun rises out of the Underworld and turns the sky orange, Kin (KEEN) tries to cover his head with his blanket and go back to sleep. But he knows it's no use, because his mother is already calling to him, "Kin! It's time to get up!"

Kin—his name means "Sun"—is a twelve-year-old Lacando'n boy. He lives with his family in a house with a cement floor and a big red door in the town of Palenque (Pah LANE kay), Mexico.

While Kin gets dressed, his mother, Margarita, turns on the light in the kitchen. She asks Kin to go out into the yard and get some eggs for breakfast.

"Do I have to?" Kin asks.

"Only if you want to eat."

The day is already getting hot as Kin walks under the banana plants. The chickens scatter when they see him coming to get their eggs. He reaches into the coop and picks out the best eggs, holding them up to the light to make sure that they're not rotten. Then he takes them back to the house, where the rest of the family is waking up.

While his mother cooks breakfast, Kin helps his grandmother take care of the family's new puppy. Then he joins his grandfather, who is waiting for his *pozole* (po SOH lay), a hot corn drink that he enjoys every morning. Grandfather is wearing a white tunic, which is the traditional clothing of the Lacando'n Indians, who once roamed the green forests around Palenque. Grandfather remembers the old ways of his people. When he talks to Kin, he uses the Maya language. Kin understands his grandfather because he also speaks Maya. But he prefers to speak Spanish, which is the national language of Mexico. Kin would like to cut his hair short like other Mexican boys, but his father won't let him because it's traditional for the Lacando'n to wear their hair long.

Kin has never shown much interest in the old Maya traditions. But now that Kin is twelve, his father, Chan Kin, feels that he's ready to begin learning the ancient ways. Chan Kin is an artisan who sells his wares to tourists at the pyramids outside of town. Kin would rather be out playing soccer, but he reluctantly agrees to stay home and help his father make the ceremonial clay figures.

Using clay that comes from a special place in the jungle, Chan Kin expertly molds a figure. In a few minutes his fingers have turned the ball of clay into a little man with thick arms and legs. Kin picks the man up, and the small eyes seem to be staring back at him.

Seeing that Kin is interested, his father tells him to sit down and pay attention. "You make a picture here," Chan Kin says, pointing to his head. "And then you let your fingers do the work."

After the figures are formed, Kin's father lets them dry for a month. Then, when the time is right, he builds a fire and puts the figures into the hot coals to bake.

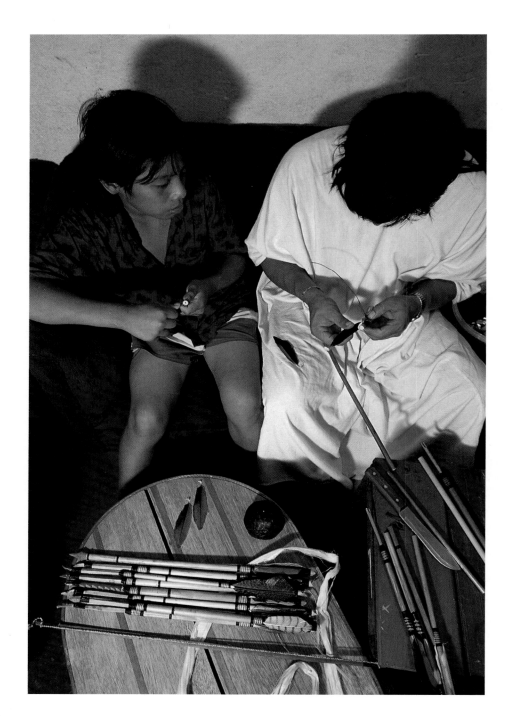

While they're baking, Chan Kin shows his son how to make hunting arrows with parrot feathers and stone tips. Using a steel knife, he carefully splits the bamboo shaft and ties on the flint blade with wire. Then he glues on the feathers, and the arrow is ready to be tested.

"The arrows and clay figures are part of our past," Kin's father says. "It's important to keep our aim true, even if the world has changed."

Kin's father goes out into the yard and puts a new arrow into his bow. His target is a tree about twenty yards away. He pulls back on the bow, takes aim, and—*boing!*—the arrow flies through the air. Kin's father laughs because he has missed the target. He tries again; this time the arrow sticks in the tree.

Chan Kin explains how their ancestors used bows and arrows to hunt for food, and how they placed clay statues inside the pyramids to honor their gods.

That night, Kin's grandfather shows him a book about the pyramids that tells about a king named Pacal (pah CAHL), which means "Shield." Like all Maya kings, Pacal had the power to speak to the gods through dreams and sacred visions.

Pacal was twelve years old—the same age as Kin—when he became the king of Palenque. He ruled for sixty-seven years and built many pyramids. His tomb is buried deep inside the pyramid called the Temple of Inscriptions.

"I wish I could see Pacal's tomb," Kin says.

"You can," his grandfather replies. "The tomb is open for the tourists every day. Tomorrow is Saturday. Ask your father to take you to the ruins with him, and you can visit Pacal's tomb yourself."

Kin is up extra early the next morning. At first, his father is surprised to see him waiting by the family's Volkswagen van, but when Kin explains that he wants to see Pacal's tomb his father smiles and tells him to jump in. It only takes a few minutes to drive through town and past the statue that marks the turn-off leading to the ruins, but to Kin it seems like forever. At last they arrive at the pyramids, but there are too many trees for Kin to see anything. Kin's father parks the van in the parking lot, and Kin helps him carry the boxes of arrows he has brought to sell to an area near the entrance gate. Then his father buys him a ticket and tells him he'll be waiting to drive him home. "I knew that one day you'd come," Kin's father says proudly. Still, Kin feels a twinge of sadness at seeing his father sell trinkets to tourists at the gates of the great city that his ancestors once ruled.

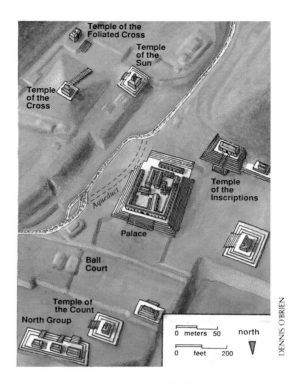

DENNIS O'BRIEN

Passing through the gate, Kin follows a tree-covered path to a plaza surrounded by incredible buildings. The pyramids are so tall that he has to bend his head all the way back to see the tops. Some of the pyramids are still half-covered by the jungle, and others have steps like long ladders leading up the sides. It took the Maya hundreds of years to build the pyramids with stones that they cut from solid rock and carried through the jungle.

Kin goes to the base of one of the tallest pyramids, the Temple of the Cross, and starts to climb. It's hard work going up the steep stairs in the hot sun. But step by step Kin climbs higher and higher, until he finally makes it to the top.

There's a small temple at the summit, and Kin goes inside to look for the inscriptions that will lead him to Pacal's tomb. But all he finds is a faded mural of a Maya priest. Kin wonders if the priest once sat in this very temple and prayed to the gods. What if Kin spoke to the gods now? Would they hear him?

Kin remembers what his grandfather told him about the great ceremonies performed by the Maya kings. Wearing costumes made from jaguar skins and bird feathers, the kings and their priests would burn strips of bark paper sprinkled with their own blood. This ritual was considered a link to the supernatural, and helped them communicate with their gods and their ancestors. Afterward, the kings would address the people, who were gathered in the plaza below, and announce what the great spirits had said. There were also ceremonies to mark the important days of the calendar, the beginning of the corn harvest, and declarations of war.

From the Temple of the Cross, Kin can see the crumbling tops of several other pyramids. When the Maya lived here, the temples were covered in smooth stucco cement and painted bright red. But by the late nineteenth century, when the pyramids were rediscovered by British and American explorers, they were almost completely covered by the jungle. Since then, Mexican archaeologists have excavated and reassembled some of the largest buildings, but most of the city remains buried under the trees and plants that thrive in Palenque's tropical climate. By studying the monuments and ancient buildings of the Maya, scientists have been able to learn a great deal about their gods and customs. Yet many aspects of the Maya culture remain a mystery and may never be fully understood.

The next pyramid Kin climbs is the Temple of the Sun. It has a wide staircase, and there are four thick pillars holding up the roof. There are inscriptions inside, but no tomb. Kin thinks about Pacal when he became king of a mighty empire. Holding out his arms, Kin pretends that he is the King of Palenque and that all the tourists below him are his subjects.

If he were really king, what would he do? He would live in the palace, of course. Bounding down the stairs, Kin crosses a trickling creek to a large building in the center of a grassy plaza.

Zigzagging down the path, he crosses the bridge over the creek and passes through an opening in the thick palace walls. Then he enters a courtyard surrounded by columns as thick as tree trunks. Kin lies on his back and looks up at the sky, trying to guess if Pacal ever played hide-and-seek here when he was a young king. Those large carved heads over there—are they pictures of Maya priests or of the Sun Gods? The faces look familiar: Their wide noses and high cheekbones remind him of his own family.

As Kin continues into the palace, he wanders through a maze of stairways and underground passages. It's so confusing. Maybe he should have joined one of the official tour groups. There are lots of tiny rooms and windows to peek through. Some of the rooms were used for sacred ceremonies; others were bedrooms for the king and his many servants.

Why are these windows shaped like a T? No one can say for sure.

Kin notices that some of the carvings have symbols mixed with pictures. He runs his fingers over the strange shapes. Are they words? Kin remembers his grandfather telling him that the ancient Maya had their own written language. He wishes he could read it.

Now Kin decides to climb the square tower at the south end of the palace.

As he walks through the different chambers and long halls, Kin sees another face carved in stone. It looks like a woman. Could this be Pacal's mother, Lady Zak-Kuk?

Kin is almost to the tower now, but first he has to jump over a gap in a wall and climb up a narrow stairway to a room with views on every side. A breeze blows through the wide windows, cooling him off. It feels good to relax and look out over the pyramids to the plains of Tabasco many miles away. The tower was probably used by Maya astrologers to track the movements of the moon and the stars, but it might also have served as a defensive lookout for enemy armies. From his perch, Kin spots yet another pyramid. Could this be the one that holds Pacal's tomb?

Kin runs down the stone steps, over the walls, and onto the plaza at the base of the pyramid. The top looks very far away. Kin starts to climb, one step at a time. One . . . two . . . three . . . four . . . five . . . Kin counts forty steps before he has to stop and rest. And he's not even there yet!

It takes a few more minutes for Kin to reach the temple at the top. The walls inside are covered with Maya writing and symbols. Could this be the Temple of the Inscriptions?

A man with a camera is peering into several holes in the floor about the size of a man's fist.

"Do you know what they are?" the man asks.

Kin doesn't.

"Those are portholes to the tomb of Pacal," the man says. "The priests of Palenque used them to speak to the dead king. It was like a telephone to the Underworld. Can you imagine!"

"Excuse me, did you say Pacal's tomb?" Kin asks.

"Yes. It's down there, all right." The man points to a stairwell that goes down into a long tunnel. "Just make sure to watch your step."

As Kin climbs down the stairs, the light makes spooky shadows on the walls. The stone steps, worn smooth by the centuries, are slippery under Kin's feet, and he has to be careful not to trip as he goes deeper and deeper into the heart of the pyramid.

The farther down Kin goes, the darker it gets—and the more nervous Kin gets—until he reaches a stone door shaped like a giant slice of pie. The door has been swung open, revealing the entrance to a small room. This must be the tomb of Pacal. But Kin hesitates. What if Pacal's body is still there? Or his ghost?

Kin forces himself to approach the threshold and look in. Suddenly he's not afraid anymore. There's no body, just a giant stone slab, which served as the lid of Pacal's coffin. In the middle of the slab, which is decorated with drawings of Palenque's kings and royal family, is a picture of Pacal.

Kin looks at the tomb for a long time, marveling at the beauty of the carvings. The symbols and drawings tell the story of Pacal, who received the crown of Palenque from his mother in 615 A.D. He ruled until the age of eighty and was buried in this very spot.

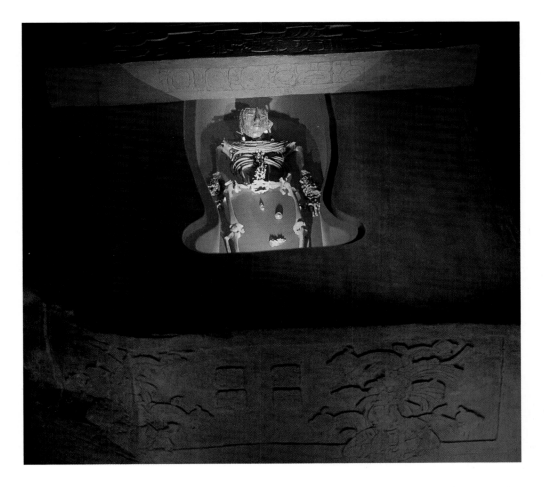

His grave was decorated with beautiful pottery and jewelry made from gold and precious stones. Many years later, archaeologists discovered the tomb and moved Pacal's bones and many other objects to a museum near the ruins.

Afterward, Kin walks over to the Palenque museum, where he learns that Pacal was part of a long dynasty of rulers that lasted until the reign of Snake-Jaguar II, who died in 702 A.D. Pacal's jade-covered skeleton and death mask are on display in the National Museum of Anthropology in Mexico City.

As Kin leaves the museum, he feels a stab of sorrow. He climbs to the top of a nearby ruin, but doesn't feel the same excitement he felt before. He knows now that he will never meet Pacal or the amazing Maya who built these pyramids. Kin wishes that he could travel back in time to visit the city during the height of its imperial glory.

Kin's father is waiting for him near the entrance to the ruins. When he asks Kin how he liked the pyramids, Kin tells him that they made him feel lonely and that he never wants to come back.

Chan Kin doesn't say anything, but Kin can tell that his father is disappointed.

Kin's father drives home silently. Then, without explaining why, he parks near the traffic circle that leads into town. In the center of the circle is a large statue of a man's head. Kin has looked at it a thousand times without knowing who it was, but now he recognizes it as the face of Pacal.

Kin runs out to get a closer look at the statue. It looks just like him! Suddenly, he understands why his father has brought him here. Even though he and Pacal live in worlds that are centuries apart, they are still brothers. Their skin and features are the same, and the same Maya blood runs in their veins.

As Kin and his father head home, he sees everything through new eyes. His Maya ancestors no longer seem so distant, and he no longer feels alone. Because, for the first time in his life, he knows how it feels to be a king.

WHAT HAPPENED TO THE MAYA?

The Maya civilization, which dates back to 2000 B.C., flourished in the jungle for nearly 3,000 years. Then, because of war or overpopulation—or some combination of both—the cities collapsed and the culture entered a period of steady decline. After the Spanish conquest of the Americas in the sixteenth century, many Maya were forced to work as slaves on Spanish *haciendas*. Some Maya rebelled against their masters and were killed. Others fled into the Lacondo'n Forest, where they learned to survive by hunting and fishing in the crystal rivers.

Today an estimated 1.2 million Maya still live in the Mexican state of Chiapas, and nearly 5 million more are spread throughout the Yucatán Peninsula and the cities and rural communities of Belize, Guatamala, Honduras, and El Salvador. The majority are poor and lack access to education, electricity, and running water. Recently Maya rebels in Chiapas started fighting to improve conditions for the Indians in southern Mexico. The government has agreed to help make their lives better, but many Maya are still angry, and it may be years before both sides can agree to a just and lasting peace.

FOR WILLIAM GARCIA

AND FOR THE

NATIVE CHILDREN

OF CHIAPAS

✸

—G. G. AND T. W.

First published in the United States of America in 1995
by Walker Publishing Company, Inc.
Published simultaneously in Canada by Thomas Allen
& Son Canada, Limited, Markham, Ontario

Library of Congress Cataloging-in-Publication Data
Garcia, Guy, 1955–
Spirit of the Maya : a boy explores his people's mysterious past
/ Guy Garcia ; photographs by Ted Wood.
p.   cm.   Includes bibliographical references.
ISBN 0-8027-8379-1. — ISBN 0-8027-8380-5 (reinforced)
1.   Lacando'n Indians—Social life and customs—Juvenile literature.
2.   Mayas—Kings and rulers—Juvenile literature.   3.   Mayas—
Antiquities—Juvenile literature.   4.   Palenque Site (Mexico)—
Juvenile literature.   5.   Palenque (Chiapas, Mexico)—Social life
and customs—Juvenile literature.   6.   Palenque (Chiapas, Mexico)—
Antiquities—Juvenile literature.   [1.   Lacando'n Indians—Social
life and customs.   2.   Indians of Mexico—Social life and customs.
3.   Mayas—Antiquities.   4.   Palenque Site (Mexico)]
I.   Wood, Ted, 1955–   ill.   II.   Title.
F1221.L2G37   1995
972'.75—dc20   94-44813   CIP   AC

Printed in Hong Kong

2   4   6   8   10   9   7   5   3   1

FOR FURTHER READING

Baquedano, Elizabeth. *Aztec, Inca and Maya*. Knopf, 1993.
Greene, Jacqueline D. *The Maya*. Franklin Watts, 1992.
Hooper-Trout, Lawana. *The Maya*. Chelsea House, 1991.
McKissack, Patricia. *The Maya*. Children's Press, 1987.
Odijk, Pamela. *The Mayas*. Silver Burdett Press, 1990.
*Schele, Linda, and David Friedel. *A Forest of Kings:
The Untold Story of the Ancient Maya*. Morrow, 1990.
Sherrow, Victoria. *The Maya Indians*. Chelsea House, 1993.
*Stephens, John L. *Incidents of Travel in Central America, Chiapas,
and the Yucatan*, Volumes 1 and 2. Dover, 1969.
Tutor, Pilar. *Mayan Civilization*. Children's Press, 1993.

*Indicates books suitable for more advanced readers.